SNOWBOARDING
KNOW-HOW

SNOWBOARDING
KNOW-HOW

CHRISTOF WEISS

Sterling Publishing Co., Inc. New York

Photo Credits
All photos are Rad Air, except
those on the following pages:
Fire & Ice, 24, 25
Kalak & Bohm, 10
North Sails, 9
Quicksilver, 8, 13
Raichle, 23
Reusch, 24
SWIX, 26, 27
Technical University of
Munich BASiS Institute, 21

Demonstrators
Daniel "Kiwi" Meier
Patrik Hasler
Michael Fruh
Reto Lamm
Sabine Wehr

Library of Congress Cataloging-in-Publication Data

Weiss, Christof.
  [Snowboarding know-how. English]
  Snowboarding know-how / Christof Weiss.
    p.   cm.
  Includes bibliographical references and index.
  ISBN 0-8069-0502-6
  1. Snowboarding.   I. Title.
GV857.S57W45   1993
796.9—dc20   93-4748
                                              CIP

Translated by Annette Englander

10 9 8 7 6 5 4 3 2 1

Published 1993 by Sterling Publishing Company, Inc.
387 Park Avenue South, New York, N.Y. 10016
Originally published in Germany and © 1992 by
BLV Verlagsgesellschaft mbH, München
English translation © 1993 by Sterling Publishing Company
Distributed in Canada by Sterling Publishing
% Canadian Manda Group, P.O. Box 920, Station U
Toronto, Ontario, Canada M8Z 5P9
Distributed in Great Britain and Europe by Cassell PLC
Villiers House, 41/47 Strand, London WC2N 5JE, England
Distributed in Australia by Capricorn Link Ltd.
P.O. Box 665, Lane Cove, NSW 2066
Printed and bound in Hong Kong
All rights reserved

Sterling ISBN 0-8069-0502-6

PREFACE

Snowboarding has been experiencing a boom the extent of which has been duplicated by very few other sports. In ever increasing numbers, people have become fascinated by the elegance and dynamics of this sport. The harmony of the movement and the intensive feeling of gliding give snowboarding an exceptional character.

The times when snowboarders were smiled at are definitely over. From a sport which was once enjoyed by only a very small group of people, snowboarding has grown and developed into a serious sport with international professionals. Snowboarding thrives on the human passion for gliding. The sport has also enriched spectators of the alpine world of winter sports because of its swings, which can reach the extreme sloping position, and its spectacular jumps. Snowboarding in deep snow is one of the most beautiful gliding experiences of winter sports. Recognizing the thrills, larger numbers of skiers have discovered snowboarding as an alternative. The direct contact with snow and the play with the forces of gravity open up new perspectives to the snowboarder.

This book is not to be viewed strictly as an instruction manual but as an attempt by the author to shed some light on the diversity of this wonderful sport. The individual sections on snowboarding are explained and described. Those who are newcomers to snowboarding will find starting easier; for the advanced snowboarder, this book offers many tips and suggestions for new maneuvers. The reader will find out about the difficulties, and how they are solved. The text, in combination with the photo sequences of individual movements, offers a good basis for learning to succeed. A glossary of snowboard terms is included at the end of the book.

Allow me, at this point, to express my thanks to those who made this book possible. First, I want to thank Paul Gruber and Harry Gunz of Rad Air Snowboarding Research & Development for their cooperation. In addition, I thank the members of the Rad Air Team for their endless patience and for the inexhaustible pleasure they take in snowboarding.

Special mention goes to Daniel "Kiwi" Meier, who performed all the alpine turns for the photos with great enthusiasm. Reto Lamm, Micky Früh, Patrik Hasler, and Sabine Wehr were responsible for the photos on the ski run, jumping hill, and in the halfpipe. Special thanks go to Micky Früh, who helped me with good tips. Thank you, Micky! Peter Mathis was responsible for the unique photos. Finally, I want to thank the companies Fire & Ice, North Sails, Quicksilver, Reusch, Swix at the BASiS Institute of the TÜV Product Service GmbH, and the professors at the Technical University of Munich for their friendly support.

CONTENTS

INTRODUCTION
The dream of gliding

What induces thousands to go to the mountains and step on the board, which becomes addictive? The magic word is "gliding." Throughout history, people have not been able to resist the temptation to experience this feeling. For the earliest inhabitants of Hawaii, riding on waves provided an unsurpassed source of fascination. Creative minds discovered new ways to experience and to perfect this feeling.

Gliding is also a way of getting in touch with life. The direct contact with water, wind, and snow conveys not only the presence of nature's forces, but also an unreal feeling, moving between floating and falling.

Another fascination for humans is the experience of speed. Whether it is high-speed distances, in the case of windsurfing; the tubes, reaching a height of 25 feet (7 m), in the case of surfing; or the wide slopes, in the case of snowboarding, the ecstasy is always there.

The close connection between snowboarding and skateboarding is obvious. Unconstrained spontaneity and constant experimenting with new tricks are characteristics of both sports. Snowboarding is not only a means of transportation on snow, it is also—this might sound exaggerated—a way of life.

Because of the individuality and diversity, it is not sufficient to describe snowboarding by comparing it to other gliding sports. There are two main fields in the sport of snowboarding. One is called alpine gliding; the other one, freestyle. The two disciplines require different attitudes and physical requirements. Because of these differences, it is possible for everyone to find the "right" style.

Alpine gliding demands a high degree of conditioning and a feeling for the edge. In no other field of this sport do gliding dynamics and speed come into play to such an extent. Extreme positions in curves, radical maneuvers, testing the edges to the extreme until one touches the snow completely—these provide endless fascination and convey a never-before-experienced play with the physical forces. The emphasis of the alpine boarder is on carving a granular, gripping ski run, on riding down a slope covered with untouched deep snow, and on the fight with the poles. Especially for the skier interested in snowboarding, this variation is of the utmost importance. The switch from skis to a snowboard is easily accomplished, since the skier already has a feeling for the edge and for speed.

Snowboarding is not just for kids. Especially in alpine boarding, it is possible to start at any age.

Freestyle is the second field of snowboarding. Just as in skateboarding, this is the discipline of individualists. The snowboarder has to focus his entire concentration on the board in order to be able to execute the most difficult tricks. There is no doubt that gliding in a halfpipe presents the greatest fascination for the freestyler. A high degree of coordination and conditioning is required of the glider. In alpine gliding, constant training and repetition of swing forms until they become perfect ensure success. In freestyle, it is the new tricks and the risks that come with them that challenge the snowboarder. The different characteristics of the two disciplines are also evident in today's professional sport. Training in alpine racing without a coach is almost unimaginable today. Spontaneity and lack of constraint, on the other hand, are expressed in the training of the freestyler. He creates his own tricks and practices them with like-minded people.

A comment on fashion: Whether colorful, very casual, or rather toned down, what you wear doesn't matter. When you snowboard you can wear whatever you like, but don't forget that clothing does not make you a world champion!

Finally, it is up to every snowboarder to act responsibly and present this sport in a good light to move one day from minority to an important place in the alpine world of winter sports.

HISTORY

Tracing our roots

Everything began, as so often happens, in the land of unlimited possibilities. By the beginning of the sixties, surfers and skateboarders already realized that the winter caused a problem for their sports. Only the fanatics went into the ice-cold surf or onto the streets. The others had to find a sport which resembled the movements of surfing and skateboarding. In the mid sixties in Muskegon, Michigan, Shermann Poppen was looking for a toy for his children. He screwed two skis together, but he did not make the connection between surfing or skateboarding and his invention. It dawned on him when he realized that his children preferred to place their feet diagonally on the board. Soon the screwed together skis were replaced by a wider pair of water skis. The "snurfer" was created. Poppen bought more water skis and worked on improving his device. He registered the product name and gave the production rights to a manufacturer of bowling balls. The first snurfers were sold

during the winter of 1966–67. Sales exceeded 100,000.

In 1968, Jake Burton Carpenter, 14 years old at the time, got hold of one of these ludicrous boards. The boy from the East Coast participated in the yearly snurf championship in Michigan. Carpenter, an enthusiastic surfer and skier, quickly detected several problems. For example, because there were no foot fastenings, the snurfer was wobbly, and the pleasure of gliding lasted only for a short while.

Carpenter began to develop his own construction. In order to create a tight connection to the board, he attached adjustable foot loops to his board. The first long downhill runs were now possible, and there was less to fear with risky maneuvers on jumping hills. Although his device began as a toy, Jake Burton Carpenter quickly saw the development of a new winter sport. In 1977, he decided to realize the dream of his own company in Vermont. The first products, though, did not sell very well. Nevertheless, Carpenter was aware of the fact that snowsurfing was an excellent alternative to alpine skiing. Other people were also active in the new field. Dimitrije Milovich was a fanatic surfer from the East Coast. In 1969 and 1970, he produced a molded polyester board. In 1972, Milovich, now living in Utah, registered his first patent. The method of construction he used was based on the construction of surfboards, and it only lasted for a short time. In 1975, he founded his own company and began to produce series boards. The so-called winter sticks, with their V-shaped cutouts in the rear (swallowtails), their fiberglass lamination, and special surface, became the first technically developed boards. Unfor-

tunately, the costly method of construction and design ate up incredible amounts of money, and the boards became, at a price of $225, a dream that nobody could afford. In 1984, Milovich finally went bankrupt.

Tom Sims, who was skateboard world champion and the star of the scene at that time, was probably the best-known snowsurf pioneer. He had been living on the West Coast since 1969, and he had dedicated his life to surfing and skateboarding. Together with Chuck Barfoot, he began to shape surfboards and, later on, to design skateboards. In the mid seventies, Sims developed his first snowboards, which were very similar to the winter sticks of Milovich. Only two years later, he switched to the laminated method with a wooden core. In the spring of 1981, the first snowboard championship took place in Colorado.

Sims won the slalom run with his new steel edges, which were laminated to his board.

Because of the high standards of safety on the part of American authorities and insurance companies, snowsurfing was taboo on American slopes, which had ski lift facilities. Snowsurfers had to climb up the slopes, a very fatiguing exercise referred to as "hiking." At that time, hiking developed into a key word for snowsurfers. It furthered the bond among the participants by forcing them to completely identify themselves with the sport.

Sadly, the first enthusiasm, which had resulted in the establishment of many companies, ended in bankruptcy for most of these firms. Only Jake Burton and Tom Sims survived the downs of the tough snowsurfing business. With the development of the shell binding and the technical refinement of

the board, the objections of the authorities and insurance companies were removed. By the mid eighties, the snowboard, as we know it today, had been created. At American winter resorts, nothing stood in the way of the triumphant advance of this sport.

When the skateboard wave hit Europe, interest in the new gliding sport began to grow also. The former Swiss champion of skateboarding, Jose Fernandez, was instrumental in developing interest in the sport. He was the first European to race against the American snowboard pros in Calgary.

The first snowboard contests were now in Europe. Fernandez won. He used a rebuilt ski-touring binding. By doing so, he set new standards, which influenced the development of snowboarding in Europe. Enthusiasm for the new sport increased slowly but continuously in Europe. In 1986, the first snowboard camp took place in Livigno. Contests and training camps were organized everywhere throughout the Alps. In 1987, the first world championships took place in Europe in Livigno and St. Moritz. Snowboarding arrived in the limelight of the media and advertising for the first time.

In 1987, the International Snowboard Association (ISA) was established. Its goal was to organize the snowboard sport internationally. After that, the first national snowboard associations were founded. Teaching methods were developed, and the training of snowboard teachers was begun. By the end of the eighties, a fully-organized professional sport with sponsored teams existed. In America, the driving forces of snowboarding were to be found mostly in the surf and skateboard scene. In Europe, however, parallel to the skateboard scene, a completely new group of snowboarders was established, which developed the so-called "Eurocarving." This refers to the extreme alpine gliding style, which developed due to the enormous progress in board materials. Gliders from this circle are usually good former skiers, who discovered a new challenge in snowboarding, and who want to experience alpine skiing (including speed, icy slopes, extreme usage of the edges, and pole skiing) from a new perspective. They usually glide with a plate binding, ensuring an optimal transfer of forces. As already mentioned, the development of the freestyle field was determined by the surf and skateboard pros from America. Many of them switched and became snowboard freestylers. They transferred the sequence of movements from their former sport to snowboarding. Already possessing a perfect feel for tricks, the American pros were guaranteed predominance in the freestyle contests right from the beginning. Today, the competitive field covers three main disciplines. Besides the suspenseful parallel slalom and the super G races, the halfpipe developed into what is probably the most spectacular competitive discipline. But the fact that the gliding techniques and the tricks matured so quickly, would not have been possible without the rapid development of high-tech-boards.

Board

The development of today's snowboards makes it possible for manufacturers to offer the right board for each discipline, similar to what ski manufacturers do. As a result, a person interested in snowboards is confronted with an almost overwhelming diversity of product. This diversity often completely confuses beginners.

Snowboards can be divided into three main groups:

★ All-around boards

EQUIPMENT
For snowboard use only!

★ Alpine race boards
★ Freestyle boards
Three different methods of construction are used:
★ Foam method (injection method)
★ Compound method
★ Sandwich method with wooden core

Using the foam method, manufacturers can produce inexpensive boards. The foam is pressed under high pressure into a form. Other construction parts are foamed in at the same time.

The second method of construction, the compound method, has a wooden core that is covered with glue and surrounded by foam. The problem with this method involves fixing the wooden core during the foaming process. But if the method is mastered properly, characteristics similar to the ones of the

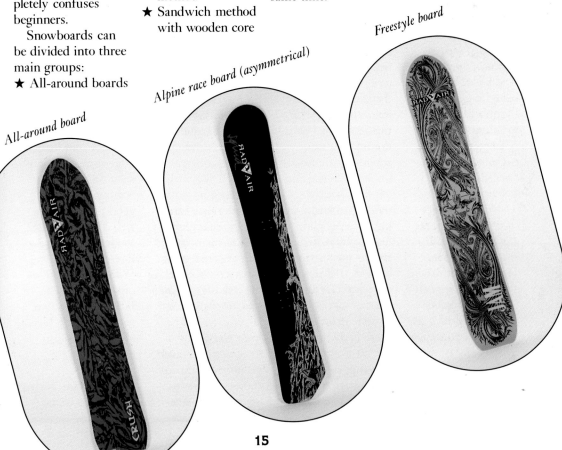

Freestyle board

Alpine race board (asymmetrical)

All-around board

laminated board are achieved.

The most expensive method is the laminated sandwich method. In this procedure, all construction parts are coated with a resin base and forced together under high pressure at a prescribed temperature. These products are unsurpassed in their longevity and their quality. Additional structural characteristics, which add to the high quality of this board are:

★ Steel-edges inserted very precisely and mounted with rubber
★ Bumper guard, laminated onto the board at the nose and tail
★ Perfectly sanded sole and perfect workmanship of the side cheeks
★ Anti-glide pad made of rubber in the area between the binding, which enables the snowboard to ride up the ski-lift without any problems (absolutely necessary!)

Two different procedures for mounting the bindings are offered by the manufacturers:

★ The binding is screwed into brass inserts which are inserted into the boards
★ The binding is screwed into the snowboard in the binding area with special screws

There are a number of construction characteristics that affect the gliding qualities of a board. These are discussed separately below.

Tension span

As is the case with skis, the snowboard is bent upwards slightly in the binding area. Thus, the edges only grip when pressure is applied by the glider. A high tension span ensures a good grip on ice, but this is a disadvantage for turning capacity. Less tension span, on the other hand, improves the turning capacity but impairs the grip of the edges on a hard slope.

Bending curve and hardness

The bending curve, the distribution of elasticity on the board, and the hardness of the board have different effects on gliding qualities. A medium-hard board offers a good grip on the ice and a high degree of gliding steadiness. Harder boards have a higher degree of stiffness, resulting in a better grip on the ice. A board that is soft in the shovel area or a board that is soft throughout has enhanced turning capacity, but this is accomplished at the expense of gliding steadiness and edge grip.

Waisting

The distance between the widest spot of the nose and tail, in other words, the maximal depth of the waisting, is decisive for the strength of the board. The most waist there is, the better the board's performance in curves and its reaction to the smallest

changes in movement.

Effective edge length

This is the part of the edge which actually grips the surface. A longer effective edge length results in a better ice grip.

Sole

The sole of the board consists of a polyethylene coating. The least expensive boards have coats with little wax-absorbing capacity. The vitreous and doubly vitreous coats have a very large sphere of temperatures for different types of snow and a large capacity to absorb wax. Graphite coatings have very good gliding qualities. They are softer, though, and therefore more sensitive. With the exception of some freestyle boards, which have a slightly convex sole, all boards have a level sole.

Nose and tail forms

The forms of the

nose and tail are determined by the respective area in which the board is used. Nose forms with a relatively large shovel radius are meant for all-around and freestyle boards. The alpine race boards, on the other hand, have a short, flat shovel, in order to achieve an edge length which is as effective as possible. Apart from the special tail forms of the freestyle board, two versions of the all-around freestyle board are available:

★ The square tail (straight back) with a good edge grip in the curve
★ The rounded square tail (rounded tail and tailkick), which allows for gliding
In addition, there is the so-called swallowtail with its cut in the back. It is always used for gliding in deep snow. The so-called asymmetrical boards occupy a special position. With this method of construction, the different pressure points

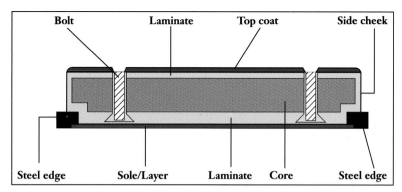

Board cross section showing different parts.

on the frontside and backside, which appear on symmetrical boards, are supposed to be balanced. Originally used for racing, the asymmetrical board developed into the most popular of the alpine boards.

There are three different methods of construction for the asymmetrical board: The simplest and at the same time most affordable solution is a board with a symmetrical shovel and a longer, waist-fitting backside edge. The disadvantage, which is the result of the

Top and side view of a snowboard

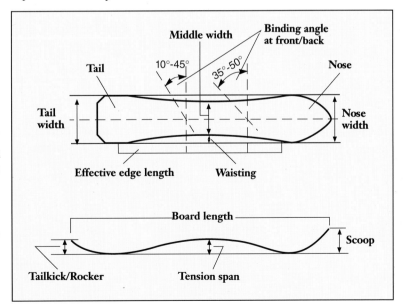

two different edge lengths, is removed through a further method of construc- tion. This is accomplished by shifting the backside edge up to a maximum of 3 inches (8 cm) and by inserting a straight piece in between. But the best solution to the problem is a complete shifting of the board lengthwise with a diagonal

Target group	Board characteristics	Area to be used	Gliding skills
All-around boards for beginners	Length: 60–65 inches (150–165 cm); soft to medium hard; medium waisting; little tension span; tailkick; large shovel radius	Alpine, as well as freestyle; flat, well-prepared slopes, at low speeds	Few gliding skills; no experience necessary
All-around boards for advanced snowboarders	Length: 61–65 inches (155–165 cm); medium hard; medium to strong waisting; medium tension span; little tailkick; medium shovel radius; may be asymmetrical	All-around alpine oriented or all-around freestyle oriented; all snow or slope conditions at medium speeds	Advanced skills; mastery of the drift-swing forms, of the basic cut swing and of easy freestyle tricks
Freestyle/halfpipe boards	Length: 55–63 inches (140–160 cm); soft to medium hard; low waisting; low tension span; strong nose/tailkick; large shovel radius; wide tail; short effective edge length 31–47 inches (80–120 cm)	Halfpipe; bumpy slopes; free riding; medium to steep slopes; all snow and slope conditions at low to high speeds	Gliding without compromise in the halfpipe; secure mastery of the most difficult tricks under all conditions
Alpine/race boards	Length: 61–67 inches (155–170 cm) narrow construction; medium to hard; strong waisting; medium to strong tension span; small shovel radius; long effective edge 51–53 inches (130–135 cm) asymmetrical construction	Icy slopes; bumpy slopes; slalom; medium to steep slopes; medium to very high speeds	High skills: secure mastery of all drift and cut swing forms with fast changing curve radiuses; gliding under all snow conditions

shovel. With this method, the glider stands with his heel (backside) and the tips of his toes (frontside) on the actual edge. A distribution of almost the same pressure on the frontside and backside edges is achieved.

However, the choice of a board does not only depend on the area where it is used. Body height and weight are additional criteria to be considered in the choice of a board. Heavier gliders, for example, should use longer and harder boards.

The purchase of a board depends on:
★ Gliding skills
★ Area in which it is used
★ Body weight
★ Body height

Binding

The choice of a suitable binding is much easier than the choice of the board. Two different binding systems are available for the snowboarder.

Plate binding
The plate binding is adjustable in size. This binding should be used with special, hard shoes. Most plate bindings are entered from a front fastening, which fixes the boot into the binding. Because of the relatively small mobility or flexibility in the leg area below the back binding, so-called canting wedges are installed. These allow the back leg to assume an anatomically correct position. With this binding, an optimal transfer of energy onto the board is achieved. Plate bindings are used mainly in the alpine sport.

Shell or soft binding
The shell binding is used primarily for freestyle and halfpipe. This binding is used with a soft boot and allows the glider a high degree of flexibility on the board. Two to three adjustable buckles guarantee an even distribution of pressure and attach the

Area of usage	Binding angle	
	Front	Back
All-around boards	40°–45°	35°–40°
Freestyle/halfpipe boards	35°–40°	10°–15°
Alpine/race boards	45°–50°	40°–45°

boots to the board. Paddings in the buckle and spoiler area make sure that the binding fits comfortably. The forward lean is adjusted through the spoiler. The high flexibility of the shell binding makes it possible for the glider to enjoy a real surfing experience in powder.

Safety binding
The issue of safety is gaining more and more importance in snowboarding. Most falls that have unpleasant results occur on hard and icy slopes. Turning falls (caused by the cant-

ing or twisting of the board) are the most frequent type of accident, often resulting in contusions and strains. Knee injuries are the most frequent result, followed by injuries to the ankle, wrist, fingers, shoulders, and the head. When snowboarding is done while wearing ski boots, the injuries usually occur in the knee area, including the ligaments, the cartilage, or a combination of injuries. When soft boots or snowboard shoes are worn, the area of the injuries shifts to the ankle. Strains of the outer

Body height	Binding distance
59 inches (150 cm)	15 inches (38 cm)
63 inches (160 cm)	15¼ inches (39 cm)
67 inches (170 cm)	15¾ inches (40 cm)
71 inches (180 cm)	16 inches (41 cm)
75 inches (190 cm)	16½ inches (42 cm)
79 inches (200 cm)	17¼ inches (44 cm)

ligaments and complete ligament lacerations are the most frequent injuries, but they are usually easier to treat, and they heal faster. While beginners usually injure their knees and ankles, advanced gliders have more injuries in the area of the hands, arms, and shoulders.

The main focus of the safety experts is on the connection between the shoe and the board. Divided opinions, though, still dominate the newly developed safety bindings. While safety bindings are used by beginners and advanced gliders, very good gliders and racers still have their doubts about the new binding system. However, for beginners and for somewhat older gliders, safety bindings can be used to prevent injuries. They can also help overcome the fear of injuries.

The most important requirement for a safety binding is the multidirectional

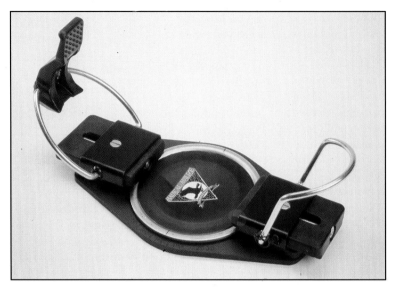

(three-dimensional) release facility. It makes sense that the front and back bindings are released separately, since the experienced glider, at low speeds, has the possibility to prevent a fall with the released leg. The safety bindings on the market fulfill the above-mentioned requirements and meet the demands of the beginning and advanced snowboarders. In the near future, snowboarding should free itself of its image as an injury-prone sport. Very good gliders and racers,

though, are still very wary of the safety system. Possible false releases at high speeds would have fatal results. For freestyle snowboarding, the safety binding is not an issue, since in this area, forces occur that would inevitably result in a false release. Therefore, there won't be a safety binding for freestyling in the near future.

Another problem involves fixing the board to the leg with the catch strap. In case of a fall, when both bindings are released, injuries inevitably occur at high

speed. Unfortunately, a stopper has not been developed yet. The discussion about the issue of safety bindings has not ended yet. In fact, manufacturers of alpine boards are being asked to find an optimal solution for everyone. But from an overall viewpoint, the risk of injury in snowboarding can be reduced if some basic rules are observed. For example, beginners should participate in a snowboarding class that includes training as well as the usage of suitable equipment.

Plate binding

Shell binding

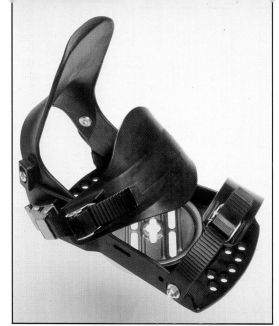

*A depiction of the digitalized
movement of the board*

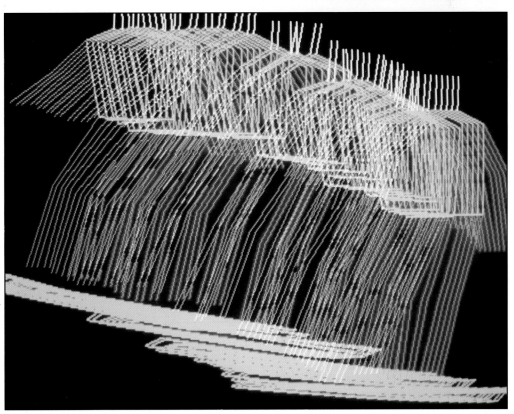

In an extensive study by the department of sports trauma at the Technical University in Munich, data was gathered with questionnaires. This information gives us more precise statistics concerning injuries. Part of the data is shown in the following tables about the risk of injury in snowboarding.

Percentage of injuries when using a shell binding		Percentage of injuries when using a plate binding	
Wrist	18.75	Knee	33.62
Knee	16.67	Wrist	12.93
Shoulder	10.42	Shoulder	8.62
Ankle	8.33	Ankle	8.62
Head	8.33	Shin	5.62
Finger	8.33	Other parts	30.59
Spine	6.25		
Hip	6.25		
Lower arm	6.25		
Other parts	8.33		

The different uses (freestyle and alpine) of the two binding systems have to be taken into consideration in the following table.

Localization of the injury in %		Type of injury in %	
Bone	37.50	Strain	54.95
Ligament	35.83	Fracture	32.43
Sinew	13.33	Laceration	9.01
Muscle	13.33	Partial laceration	3.60

Complaints of overstress in comparison to skill in %		Injuries in comparison to skill in %		Speed at fall when injury occurs in %	
Advanced	53.60	Advanced	49.37	Medium	61.65
Very capable	28.80	Very capable	31.65	Slow	21.80
Beginners	17.60	Beginners	18.99	Fast	16.54

Of those interviewed, 45.39% had injuries in their first year of snowboarding; 26.97 were injured in their second year; 21.05% in their third; and only 5.26% in their fourth year. Snow conditions play an important role in the occurrence of injuries. A large portion of injuries happened on icy (30.05%) or granular slopes (32.69%).

Shoes

For each type of binding, there is a matching boot system:

Hard boots

These are always used with plate bindings. Each boot consists of an inside and an outside shoe. Thus, a strong foothold and an optimal transfer of forces is guaranteed. The boots are adjustable in the forward lean, in the lateral flex, and in the damping of the forward lean.

A high rear or back spoiler at the inside shoe offers an additional rearward foothold. In order to prevent the shoes from jutting out on the narrow alpine boards, the boots are slanted at the front and back. Manufacturers offer systems with two or three buckles. The hard boots should fit exactly to prevent sore points from too much pressure.

Hard boot

Soft boot

Soft boots

These are the boots for shell bindings. They give the ankles the necessary freedom to move, which is needed in freestyling. Consisting of an inside and an outside shoe, the soft boot is tied and partially fixed with self-locking nylon fastenings. In order to avoid unnecessary pain, the soft boot should reach over the rear spoiler of the shell binding and should be padded sufficiently in the instep area. Just as with the hard boot, an exact fit is absolutely necessary.

Outfit

Function and fashion distinguish snow-boarding attire. With colorful sweaters in the spring and fashionably wide-cut jackets and trousers in the winter, snow-boarding has brought some pep into the fashion life of the slopes. Despite the large choice available, especially beginners (who usually suffer from a lot of wetness), should keep an eye on the functional aspects of their

outfits, including resistance to water and wind. Differences in attire become obvious only when you look at the details. Pants should have reinforcements in the knee and bottom areas. A wide crotch ensures the necessary freedom of movement. In order to be protected against the snow in falls, pants which reach over the hips with a high back and straps are recommended. Jackets should pull together at the bottom. Gloves can be a problem, because of the merciless wear and tear they receive. They should be doubly reinforced at the inside of the hand and at the fingertips. An integrated wrist protection is also an advantage. For people interested in slalom, a specially padded glove for blow protection is recommended. For the head and the shin bones, there are also special blow protectors. Although they cannot be called clothing, sunglasses, with 100 percent UV protection, are of great importance. Many "hot" glasses are available on the market.

Snowboard fashion is colorful and lively, but also functional.

Board Care

As everyone knows, with material that is well cared for, gliding is a great joy. Proper care of the board influences its gliding behavior. The sole must be level, smooth, clean, and waxed in order for the board to glide and turn well. The same care applies to the edges. Only a sharp, granular edge offers enough lead to keep the direction of the board. With only a little expenditure, you can prepare the board properly.

Sharpening the edges

Before actually sharpening the edges, hardenings and crests have to be removed with a grindstone or file. Use an edge sharpener for the lateral edges. This is done in a hanging position at an angle of 0.5 to 1°. The desired angle is set on the edge sharpener, and the bow-shaped ribs of the file are placed on it in the direction in which it is to run. With a slight pressure, the device is slowly and evenly pulled over the edge.

The side edges have to be relief-ground at a 90° angle, or, for an optimal ice-grip, use 2 to 3°.

In the next step, the angle of the edge sharpener has to be set, and the bow-shaped ribs of the file have to be placed on it in the direction in which it is to run. With a slight pressure, the device is evenly pulled over the edge. In order to avoid cutting up the board, the edges have to be correctly finished after being sharpened. To do so, draw an edge finisher along the entire length of the edge two to three times.

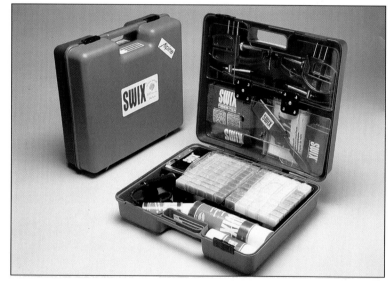

Professional waxing set

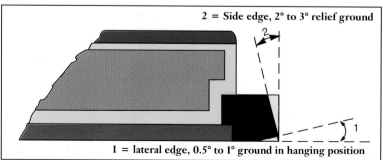

2 = Side edge, 2° to 3° relief ground

1 = lateral edge, 0.5° to 1° ground in hanging position

Cross section of an edge sharpening

26

Coating repair

To repair the coating, so-called repair strips are used. The repair strips are heated with an iron and pressed into the pre-warmed, cleaned scratch. After the board has cooled off sufficiently, the parts which jut out are removed with a car-body file. The spot is finally smoothed

with fine sanding paper. From time to time, polishing the coating on a stone-grinding machine is recommended. However, this should only be done with boards that have a planed sole.

Cleaning the coating

To clean the coating, hot (cleaning) wax is ironed onto the sole with an iron. Before it gets cold, the wax is peeled off with an acrylic blade. Chemical cleaning detergents can also be used. They are less expensive, but not as gentle on the coating.

Waxing

In order to create the desired result, the correct wax has to be chosen according to snow conditions. Due to the heat generated while gliding, little water drops are created between the

coating and the snow. The proper wax counterbalances this effect, so that an optimal relationship between the remaining friction and the humidity exists. The temperature and consistency of the snow are also taken into consideration. To help with the choice of a suitable wax, manufacturers offer

comprehensive tables that can be easily understood. In principle, waxing should be done at room temperature, guaranteeing that the coating absorbs the wax properly. The wax is applied with an iron

or a waxing device. Iron it on evenly for several minutes. Work from the shoulder to the back part. Be careful! Do not let it get too hot, only up to about 54°F (12°C). After the wax has cooled off for at least an hour, the remaining parts are carefully peeled off with an acrylic blade. To en-

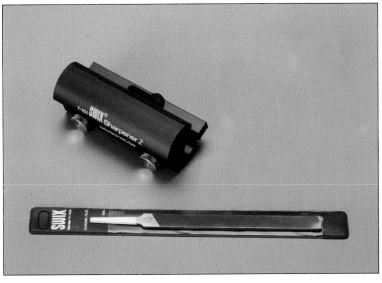

Edge sharpener with adjustable edge (to be placed on the board) and the file to finish the edges

hance the gliding performance of the board even more, add a texture to the coating by brushing with a texture brush in the longitudinal direction from the front to the back. The type of brush depends on the snow conditions:

★ Nylon brush for powdery snow
★ Copper brush for old snow or wet snow

Now, there is nothing to stop you from enjoying gliding. Let's go!

Taking that First Ride

To begin a snow-boarding day correctly, you should warm up and stretch conscientiously before stepping on the board. Fitness-training before the season (once or twice a week) is advisable. Unfortunately, warming up is often ignored by skiers as well as by snow-boarders! By warming up, the risk of injury in the sport of snowboarding is drastically reduced. Therefore, let the board rest while you warm up first. The feeling of gliding will follow!

ALPINE GLIDING TECHNIQUES
Get the feeling!

Warming up

Since a complete description of exercises would go beyond the scope of this book, the snowboarder should read *Stretching: The Quick and Easy Way*, by Dagmar Sternad and Klaus Bozdech, Sterling Publishing Co., Inc. Start the warm-up with running, bouncing, and little games, for about five minutes. Follow up by stretching the muscle groups that are stressed in snow-boarding. It is important to proceed systematically.

The following body parts should be stretched:
★ Head-arm-shoulder area
★ Wrists
★ Back and spine
★ Lateral trunk muscles
★ Bottom muscles
★ Leg muscles
★ Ankle muscles

Checking the equipment

Regardless of the fact that you checked your equipment at home, the following should be checked again before the first ride:
★ Is the catch strap fastened to the front binding?
★ Are all the binding screws tight?
★ Are the boots OK?

In snowboarding, it is important to learn the correct way to carry and put down the board. It should always be carried vertically and close to the body. The catch strap is wrapped around the wrist. The board is placed with its upper side into the snow. All other variations could have dire consequences for the other people on the slopes! A snowboard without a master can turn into a weapon.

Getting into the binding depends on the binding type—plate or shell.

Getting into plate bindings

In general, face the mountain in the case of bindings with back fastenings, and face the valley in the case of bindings with front fastenings. After placing the board on a flat spot or after

Getting into the binding

Goofy position   *Regular position*

creating a small plateau, clean all snow and ice from the bindings. The catch strap always has to be fastened to the front leg. Insert the front leg first. After removing all snow from the boot, clap the fastening against the boot. The board is secured with the back leg or by kneeling down. Apply the same procedure at the back. It is essential to re-check the fastenings of the binding and the catch strap!

Getting into shell bindings

Just as with plate bindings, one gets into shell bindings from the front. Facing the valley, the boot is fixed first with the instep buckle, then the tow buckle is fastened. The procedure is repeated for the back binding.

Basic terms

Before we get to the first exercises, let's clarify a few basic terms which appear frequently on the following pages.

Positions of the feet

There are two positions of the feet on the board. The terms come from skateboarding:

★ Regular position: left foot in the front binding

★ Goofy position: right foot in the front binding

Gliding directions

Two different gliding directions are distinguished on the board:

★ Frontside: gliding direction with face and upper body towards the hill

★ Backside: gliding direction with face and upper body towards the valley

Names of edges

The edges are

★ Frontside edge: toe edge

★ Backside edge: heel edge

Just as in skiing, we talk about a

★ Mountain edge: the board edge which is closer to the hill

★ Valley edge: the board edge which is closer to the valley

Basic position

The position from which almost all maneuvers are executed is called the basic position:

★ Upper body is turned about 45° forward.

★ Hips, knees, and ankles are bent at different degrees.

★ Body weight is distributed evenly on both legs.

★ Eyes face forward.

First exercises

The first exercises take place on level ground. Balancing exercises are especially good for getting used to the board. The starting position is always the basic position.

Basic position

Balancing exercises
★ Lowering the body and raising it in the basic position.
★ Tilting the board onto the frontside and backside edges.
★ Shifting the body's center of gravity backwards and forward.
★ A slight jump and stretch of the body, followed by a soft landing.

Falling down
The most important exercise for the beginner is to learn how to fall and get up again. Falling in a controlled way helps avoid injuries. Standing up effortlessly can save energy.

Frontside fall
If you lose your balance on the frontside edge, your upper body has to be brought to the ground as quickly as possible. This is accomplished by stretching slightly. The arms are kept at the sides. The impact is absorbed by the large surface of the upper body, arms, and upper thighs, not by the hands and knees. In the prone position, the knees are quickly bent. At the same time, the board is lifted out of the snow. Remain in this position, until you have come to a standstill.

Backside fall
If you lose your balance on the backside edge, quickly bend your knees to bring your center of gravity above the board. Again, the arms are kept at the sides. Under no circumstances should you reach back with your hands! The impact is absorbed by rolling onto your back. At the same time, lift the board out of the snow. Remain that way until you have come to a standstill.

Getting up
In order not to waste your strength when getting up, pay attention to these tips. When you get into the binding, it is sometimes easier to

get up via the frontside edge. Put pressure on the frontside edge with the tips of the toes. The upper body and the arms are brought above the frontside edge. The body is raised by pushing off the ground with the hands while straightening the knees. If you are standing on the backside edge, your front arm has to be brought close to the board. Exert pressure on the backside edge with the heels. and bring the upper body above the board. The legs and the body are lifted by swinging the back arm and pushing off the ground with the front hand.

Roller technique

The first gliding pleasure is experienced by the beginner through so-called roller riding. Here, only the front leg is in the binding. With the back leg, you alternately push or place the back foot on the anti-glide pad.

Now we go down-

Top to bottom: frontside fall, backside fall, roller technique

wards! For the next steps, look for a very flat, well-prepared, wide slope. Next on the schedule is gliding in the fall line (the imaginary line between the highest and lowest points of the slope), straight down. Out of the basic position, let the board glide into the fall line. Stay loose! The board does not go too fast, since the slope runs into a level surface! It is important that the board always points directly towards the valley.

Side sliding

The next exercise is side sliding in the fall line. The starting position is the basic position with pressure on the mountain edge. By slowly taking weight off the mountain edge, the board starts to move. Be careful! Taking too much weight off the mountain edge often results in a canting or tilting of the valley edge, resulting in a fall. In order to brake, the pressure on the mountain edge is increased.

Diagonal sliding

When sliding diagonally, the board is moved forward or backwards in the fall line. From the basic position, with pressure on the mountain edge, the pressure on the edges is released in small doses, and you shift your weight somewhat onto the front (diagonal sliding forward) or onto the back leg (diagonal sliding backwards). The exercise

31

is executed on both sides (frontside and backside).

Diagonal ride

In the diagonal ride, the beginner moves only on the edge of the board. The position of the diagonal ride is similar to that of the diagonal slide; the pressure on the mountain edge is on the frontside edge, enhanced with the toes. In the ride on the backside edge, more pressure is put on the heels. At the edge of the slope, the first change in direction takes place: simply put the board down and turn it.

Riding the lift

After several successful practices, "hiking" comes to an end for the time being. The lift is waiting. (If you ride the T-bar lift, don't use the one that goes up the steepest slope). Only the front leg remains in the binding. After the loose parts of the open back binding have been folded in, you position yourself on your best side: the regular rider to the left of the bar, the goofy rider to the right of the bar. Grab the bar and hook it under the front upper thigh or place it behind your bottom (this is more difficult for the beginner). The jerk experienced when the lift starts up is counterbalanced by leaning slightly forward. The back leg remains on the anti-glide pad during the ride. Do not cramp up during the ride. In case the lift tracks are not straight, steer the board against the incline of the slope. When getting off, pull the bar slightly with your arms and push it aside. With the help of the roller technique, quickly leave the platform. When riding a chair lift, the board should point in the direction you are moving. The same is true when getting on and getting off. Usually, the chair lift does not cause any problems.

Getting on the T-bar lift and securing the correct position for the ride

Getting on the chair lift

large number of snow-boarders still "prefers" the wrong technique for riding down the slopes. The phrase is "counter-rotation." This gliding style, which is not very appealing aesthetically, refers to the constant turn of the upper body in a direction against the swing. Although the board can be cheated around the curve quite well at low speeds, this type of gliding reaches its limits very fast at higher speeds. Uncontrolled and dangerous gliding is the result. Another disadvantage of this gliding style becomes apparent in the development of other gliding techniques. Once the mistake has become second nature, there will be a lot of frustration. It is then almost impossible to advance. Save yourself time and irritation. Learn the correct technique from the beginning!

For the following swings, it is best to pick a flat slope. The following movement descriptions refer to frontside as well as

Backside

Drift Swing

The drift swing is the first targeted change of direction on the board. It is the basis for all alpine swing forms and is executed by beginners as well as by racers. It lays the cornerstone for the development of gliding technique. Therefore, it must be practised very intensively, because a good gliding technique provides advertisement for the sport! A glance at the slopes shows what this means. Unfortunately, a

backside turns. The two swings differ in the way they look, but the technical sequence of movements is identical.

Drift swing up the slope

Swinging towards the slope is a good practice exercise for the drift swing and an important braking maneuver. The swing is started from the basic position with a slight diagonal sliding. By shifting the weight onto the front leg and by simultaneously lifting the mountain edge out of the snow, the board moves slightly in the direction of the fall line and gathers speed.

The swing is initiated with a distinct upper body and hip rotation towards the slope; the board follows. The arms remain at the sides in front of the body. By putting slight amounts of pressure on the edges, the board comes to a halt again.

Frontside

Tips

★ Shift the weight onto the front leg.
★ Execute the upper body and hip rotation towards the slope.
★ Position yourself centrally on the board.
★ Face the gliding direction.
★ At the end of the swing, put pressure on the edges in small doses.

Basic drift swing

As the name implies, this swing is the basis for all the following swings. The basic swing is initiated in the basic position from a diagonal ride. The board is brought into the fall line by shifting pressure onto the front leg and simultaneously bringing the board into a flat position. The upper body and the hips rotate in the swing direction, and the board follows. The board is canted in the fall line. By continuing to rotate the upper body and the hips, the swing can be steered. At the end of the swing, pressure is put on both legs equally. The basic position is reached again by returning to a diagonal ride.

Tips

★ Enhance pressure on the front leg.

★ Rotate the upper body and hip in the swing direction.

★ Face the gliding direction.

★ Maintain a central position on the board.

★ Cant the board only when you are in the fall line.

★ Keep steering of the swing well-balanced.

Basic swing with stretch pressure release

The basic swing with pressure release by stretching is the first swing that uses a vertical movement to initiate the swing. It is usually done on a steep slope, and it is the basis for the cut swing with pressure release by stretching. The swing is started in a strongly bent basic position. The swing starts with a distinct upper body and hip rotation in the swing direction. This is supported by stretching the body. The board, which is relieved of pressure because of the stretch movement, is canted in the fall line. As soon as the board has passed the fall line, the pressure on the edges increases gradually, and the swing is steered into a diagonal ride. Once this swing is mastered, you can go one step further and cant the board before the fall line. In this case, a dynamic stretch is absolutely necessary to ride on steep slopes.

Practice exercises for the swing:

★ Practice the combined movement (rotation and stretch) on a level slope.
★ Lower and raise the body with the knees while doing the diagonal ride.

Possible problems:

★ Difficulty in turning the board in the fall line.
★ Falling while doing the swing on the inside of the curve.
★ Oversteering the board at the end of the swing.

Tips

★ Stronger pressure on the front leg.
★ Distinct upper body and hip rotation; enhanced stretching movement; placing the board flat on the ground.
★ Face the direction of the ride.
★ Only cant in the fall line; maintain a central position on the board.
★ At the end of the swing, return to the basic position.

Basic swing with crouch pressure release

The basic swing with pressure release by lowering the body is the basis for dynamic, gliding swings which are drawn out at high speeds. At the same time, it is the basis for techniques on bumpy slopes.

Again, it starts out in the basic position. As in the basic drift swing, the board is brought into the fall line by shifting the weight onto the front leg. The swing is initiated by a distinct upper body and hip rotation in the swing direction with a quick, dynamic movement downwards. The board, relieved of pressure through the bend, is canted in the fall line. It is important to maintain a central position on the board. The body rotation continues; the swing is balanced by a stretch that is adapted to the swing radius and executed in small stages. The starting position (basic position) for the next swing is reached again. Just as with the basic swing with stretch pressure release after mastering this swing form, the board is canted before the fall line.

Practice exercises for the swing:

★ Practice the movement on level ground in a standing position.
★ Quickly lower the body in the diagonal ride.

Possible problems:

★ Difficulty turning the board in the fall line.
★ Falling during the swing on the inside of the curve.
★ Board oversteers at the end of the swing.

Tips

★ Stronger pressure on the front leg; strong upper body and hip rotation; lowering the body; placing the board flat on the ground.
★ Facing the direction of the ride.
★ Only cant in the fall line, keeping the body above the board.
★ Returning to the basic position at the end of the swing.

Cut Swing

This chapter will give you a general idea of the most fascinating and most demanding gliding technique of snowboarding, the carving. Many people have already been seized by carving fever. No matter whether it occurs on the slopes or in powder, it is a unique surfing feeling! Carving is strictly a matter of riding on the edge. Because of the high technical quality of the boards, it is possible to go into the most extreme curve positions. Looking at the slope, everyone has the desire to experience this play with the force of gravity. But carving should not be confused with senseless racing. On the contrary, it requires a high degree of feeling for movement and of control over the board. The cut swing is also used in racing, but there it occurs frequently in conjunction with short drifting.

For the following swings, a flat-to-medium-steep slope is used at the beginning. The frontside turn is done with pressure on the tip of the toe edge; the backside turn with pressure on the heel edge. The sequence of movements is the same for both turns.

Cut swing up the slope

This swing conveys a pure ride on the edge. The swing is started in the basic position out of the diagonal ride. A somewhat higher speed than in the drifted swings is necessary to cant the board. This is accomplished by shifting the body's center of gravity onto the inside of the curve. As the end of the swing approaches, the pressure on the edge is decreased. The board is brough to a halt in the basic position.

Tips

★ The swing track must be very narrow and deep; if the track is wide, the swing drifts.
★ Face the direction of the swing.
★ Ride more on the edge during swings at high speeds.
★ At lower speeds, do not position your body as strongly in the direction of the curve.

Basic cut swing

The basic cut swing is the basis for all other swing forms in alpine gliding. With this swing, you can consciously experience a sense of gliding resembling a ride on a track. The swing is started in the basic position on the mountain edge. Tilt the board onto the valley edge before the fall line is reached. This starts the swing and permits you to steer it. The position of the body in the curve and the pressure on the edge are adapted to the speed. The more you cant or tilt, the smaller the swing radius becomes. After steering out of the swing, the pressure on the edge is decreased, and the body is brought back above the board. The basic position is reached, and you can begin the next swing.

Possible problems:
* ★ The board drifts or breaks out.
* ★ Falling on the inside of the curve.

Tips

* ★ Cant stronger and earlier.
* ★ Keep body directly above the board.
* ★ For an even swing during the backside turn, turn the back shoulder in the gliding direction.
* ★ Pull the arms into the direction of the swing.
* ★ Maintain a higher speed.

Basic cut swing with stretch pressure release

This swing is very suitable for steep slopes. As with the basic drift swing with stretch pressure release, start out in the bent basic position. The board is released with a distinct stretch of the body, and it is canted before the fall line. Depending on the speed, the body is more or less bent towards the inside of the curve. A bending movement accomplished in small stages generates pressure on the edge, steering the swing until you reach the diagonal ride. In the bent basic position, the next swing can be prepared.

Possible problems:
★ Board does not turn.
★ Board breaks out after the swing is initiated.
★ Too wide track, board drifts.
★ Falling on the inside of the curve.

Tips

★ In order to initiate the swing, make a sharper upward movement.
★ Go up and afterwards down slowly.
★ Cant stronger and earlier.
★ Keep body centered above the board.
★ Turn the back shoulder forward during the backside turn.
★ Face the direction of the swing.
★ Pull arms into the direction of the swing.
★ Higher speed.

Basic cut swing with crouch pressure release

This swing is done on wide, fairly steep slopes. Racers use it frequently in the super G with an acceleration turn. Stretching the body at the end of the swing increases the acceleration of the board. Out of the basic position, the swing is initiated by quickly lowering the whole body. The pressure is removed from the board, and you cant before the fall line. The curve to the inside position depends on the speed. A slow stretch of the body follows, allowing you to steer out of the swing, and the basic position (the starting position) for the following swing is reached.

Possible problems:
★ Difficulty turning the board.
★ Too wide track, board drifts.
★ Falling on the inside of the curve.

Tips

★ To initiate the swing, lower the body further.
★ Cant stronger and earlier.
★ While steering out of the swing, stretch in small stages.
★ Keep body centered above the board.
★ Face the direction of the swing.
★ Pull the arms in the direction of the swing.
★ Turn the back shoulder in the gliding direction during the backside turn.
★ Maintain a higher speed.

Short drift swing

Short swinging is a rhythmic sequence of swings with short radii. The swings flow into each other. A diagonal ride is not used. A flat slope is recommended for practice at the beginning. The swing is initiated with an upper body and hip rotation out of the bent basic position. By briefly releasing pressure from the board while pushing up, the board is canted. Steer out by lowering the body quickly. The next swing takes place immediately in the bent position.

Possible problems:
★ Swing radii cannot be maintained.
★ Board gathers too much speed.

Tips

★ Adapt swing radii in frontside and backside turns.
★ Put more pressure on the edge at the end of the swing.

Short cut swing

As with the short drift swing, a flat slope is recommended in the beginning. This is one of the most difficult maneuvers in alpine gliding. The short cut swing demands a high degree of edge mastery and excellent conditioning. Through pressure release by raising the body, the board is tilted before the fall line onto the other edge, and after briefly lowering the body, the board is steered out. The starting position for the next swing is reached. Make sure that the swing rhythm is even and adapted to the speed.

Possible problems:
★ Swing radii cannot be maintained.
★ Board gathers too much speed.

Tips

★ Adapt swing radii in frontside and backside turns.
★ Put more pressure on the edge at the end of the swing.

Jump turn

This swing represents an extreme form of the cut high swing. It is often used on icy, steep slopes. The swing is started out of the bent basic position. After a dynamic jump from the mountain edge, the board loses contact with the snow and is canted in the air before the fall line. In landing, extreme pressure on the edge is produced. A careful lowering of the body steers out of the swing. The new swing is prepared in the bent basic position.

Possible problems:
★ Board does not lose contact with the snow.
★ Board gathers too much speed.

Tips

★ Lower the body sharply before the swing; jump more strongly from the mountain edge.
★ Enhance the pressure on the edge after the landing by lowering the body in small stages.

51

Vitelli turn

This maneuver demonstrates the play with gravity in an impressive way. The key to success in this radical turn is to get as much pressure on the edge as possible.

Starting in the basic position, the swing is initiated with a downwards movement. With the canting of the board, the body begins to tilt towards the inside of the curve. By slowly stretching the legs, an extreme pressure on the edge is produced. Almost the whole body is now lying in the snow. The swing ends when the body is forced upright and the pressure on the edge is decreased.

Techniques for bumpy slopes

Many people are afraid to glide on a bumpy slope. But, if you concentrate and don't give up after the first unsuccessful attempts, you can acquire a feeling for bumps.

There are two techniques for mastering the bumps.

Deep-bend technique

With this technique, you glide over the bumps with an up-down-up movement.

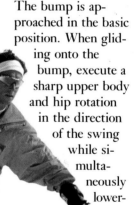

It is important to have mastered the deep-swing forms. The bump is approached in the basic position. When gliding onto the bump, execute a sharp upper body and hip rotation in the direction of the swing while simultaneously lowering the body. With the body in the lowest position, the board is released of pressure and turns on the bump into the new gliding direction. When gliding off the bump, stretch your body back into the basic position.

Hollow technique

With this technique, you ride around the bumps by lowering the body and releasing pressure. This sounds easy, but it requires just as much practice as gliding directly over the bumps. Before entering the hollow, perform a sharp upper body and hip rotation in the direction of the swing. At the same time, lower your body. This releases the pressure from the board and cants it. Afterwards, steer out by stretching your body.

Tips

★ Use flat bumps to begin.
★ Always choose the same line to practice.
★ Use rhythmic movements.

Techniques for deep snow

Depending on the area and the snow conditions, you can ride in powder using two different techniques. When riding in the backward lean position, about ⅔ of the body's center of gravity is shifted onto the back leg. This prevents the nose from dipping into the snow. The swings are initiated by shifting the body weight onto the inside of the curve. Make the turns in small stages around the back leg.

The second technique involves a simple tilting of the board in the swing direction. The weight is evenly distributed on both legs. As in the basic cut swing, no vertical movement takes place. The board is turned by the legs and hips. You get additional power by pulling the arms in the direction of the swing. Depending on the area and the snow conditions, the two techniques can be combined.

The following table shows the use of all swing forms, depending on the condition of snow and area:

Loose, powdery snow over a foot (30 cm)	In backward-lean position, steer the board through swings in small stages. The deeper the snow, the steeper the slope has to be in order to gather enough speed. Be careful falling. Getting up can be a major effort!
Loose, powdery snow up to a foot (30 cm)	Ride in the central position, as in the basic cut swing. Controlled gliding is absolutely necessary, since the ground can be icy.
Wet snow	Although awful for skiers, heavy, wet snow can be fun for snowboarders. All cut swings can be used because the edge of the board offers little resistance to the wet snow. Be careful in flat passages! Use a backward-lean position because the board can brake suddenly and powerfully.
Broken up, crushed snow	Even for snowboarders, crushed snow is torture. Use smooth, short swings with a lot of pressure. If you have mastered the jump turn, this is a good technique for this unpleasant surface.
Icy, hard slope	At controlled speeds with a balanced swing, rhythmic, cut gliding is most effective.
Steep slopes	On steep slopes, use only short swings to control the speed. You can do the short drift swing, the high cut jump, or the jump turn.
Bumpy slope	The bumpy slope is mastered with a drift swing or a deeply cut swing. The most important goal is to find a swing rhythm.

Racing: Introduction to the Pole Technique

The two alpine racing competitions are the parallel slalom and the super G. In the parallel slalom, a drop of 325 to 500 feet (100 to 150 m) is covered. The racers have to qualify in parallel, dual slaloms. The winner is determined in several parallel runs using the k.o. system. Each racer has to do both runs and fights against his competitor for the better combined time. The one with the better time enters the next round, until the last two racers compete in the finals.

The super G for snowboarders is a mix of the grand slalom and the super G. A drop of 1,150 to 2,600 feet (350 to 800 m) is covered. The course is laid out according to the area and corresponds to the natural curve-radii of free gliding. The winner is determined by one run.

Pole riding offers the non-racer a good opportunity for improving his riding technique. Because of the speed, any problems with your gliding technique become obvious, and you will want to improve your skills. Depending on the area and the layout of the course, there are different slalom techniques. On a course laid out rather rectangularly, the run is controlled with pressure release by stretching. If the course is laid out almost in the fall line, the so-called tilt turn is used. The main goal of both techniques is to go through as much of the course as possible on the edge. Most of the swings are done with mixed forms. Depending on the incline and snow conditions, short drift phases are necessary. For the slalom, rather short, medium-hard boards with a strong waist-ing and an asymmetrical shape are used. In order to avoid unnecessary bruises on the arms and legs, blow protection is recommended. The first time you go into the pole forest, choose a flat and well prepared slope. In order to get a feeling for the poles and to establish a rhythm, start with a course that has wide distances between the gates. Little by little, you can try courses that are laid out more tightly.

Slalom technique with tilt turn

The tilt turn is used in runs that are laid out close to the fall line. Do not use wide, swinging radii that employ the pressure-release technique with stretching. The gates are approached more directly. This requires a fast edge switch in which the board is tilted from edge to edge by the legs. A steady upper-body posture is especially important. The board is canted about halfway between the gates by tilting it. Immediately afterwards, the next swing is initiated. This technique should be practiced first without poles. A flat, well prepared slope is used for practice. The swings are done close to the fall line.

Practice exercise for the tilt turn (without poles)

Slalom technique with stretch pressure release

Mastering all swing forms is a prerequisite for this technique. If the gates are shifted a lot, it is necessary to cant the board by releasing pressure through stretching. It is very important to ride through the slalom course at an optimal rhythm. Keeping the upper body steady is very important. The gate is approached with the body in an upright position, and the pole is passively brushed aside with the blow protection. When passing the pole, the board is steered towards the next gate, which means that the swing should be finished at the same height as the gate. By moving into an upright position, you take pressure off of the board, and it cants. By lowering the body in small stages, you increase the pressure on the edge, and the board is steered out. Towards the end of the swing, contact with the pole takes place. By this time, the board is already headed towards the next gate. In order to find the ideal line, the boarder should have two to three gates in view. Thus, difficulties in the course can be foreseen, and a possible fall avoided.

Tips

★ Approach the gates in an upright position.
★ Exert sharp pressure release by stretching.
★ Cant immediately after passing the gate.
★ Steer the board towards the next gate.
★ Keep your movements rhythmic and maintain a steady upper body.
★ Have the gate combinations in view during the ride.

Super G gliding techniques

For speed freaks, this competition is the ultimate experience! Speeds up to 60 miles per hour (100 km/ph) are reached by the pros. In order to get used to the physical forces that are created by the speed, and in order to build up your courage, it is wise to begin with the grand slalom. Here, the gates are not laid out so widely, and the speed is reduced. For this run, medium-hard, asymmetrical boards up to 67 inches (170 cm) are recommended. As in the slalom, two techniques are used, depending on the type of the course. Passages which are laid out close to the fall line and which allow a direct approach to the gates are ridden with tilt turn. If the gates are widely shifted in a vertical direction, the ride is made with an acceleration turn.

Acceleration turn

This gliding technique consists of a pressure release by lowering the body, followed by a stretch of the body, and a slight shift of the weight towards the tail. When using this technique, it is important to approach the gates in an upright position. Coming out of the gate, the acceleration is increased by stretching the body and shifting the weight towards the tail. This is followed by a dynamic downwards movement, releasing pressure from the board, which is necessary to shift to a different edge. At the level of the gate, the board is already oriented towards the next gate. Swing steering should be used in stages during the entire course of the swing. The timed change of swings depends on the direction of the course.

In contrast to slalom, the poles should not be touched. A direct attack of the poles causes you to get out of course at high speed, and may cause a fall. For the first attempt, look for a flat slope. Because of the high speeds, don't attempt steeper slopes until you have mastered the technique.

FREESTYLE

Tricks for the slope and jumping hill

Freestyle tricks on the slope and the ramp are both playful and impressive. The inexhaustible diversity of the countryside in the alpine winter world offers endless possibilities to be creative on your board. Whether on a plain slope or on one with bumps, the freestyler uses every opportunity to play with his board. As in alpine gliding, it is important to begin with basic tricks and to slowly increase their difficulty. As already mentioned, skateboarding has greatly influenced freestyle snowboarding. Only a very few tricks were created by snowboarders. Almost all tricks come from the field of skateboarding; a small number are from surfing. Before beginning to freestyle, you should master all of the basic alpine swings. Complete control of the board is absolutely necessary. As usual, do not forget to warm up! For tricks on the slope as well as in the halfpipe, use freestyle boards with shell bindings.

Tail Wheelie

The tail wheelie is a basic trick which every freestyler should be able to master. It will improve your balance and help you feel safer on the board. A well-prepared, soft slope is suitable for your first attempts. The freestyle board should not be too hard, and it should be bent sharply upwards at the rear. Start out in the bent basic position in the fall line. By shifting your weight in fits and starts towards the back, stretching your front leg, flexing your back leg, and simultaneously raising your arms, the board is brought into the wheelie position. Now the board can be ridden on the tail. Spread your arms for balance. The advanced rider can place his arms loosely on the hips. The upper body is bent somewhat forward. In order to bring the wheelie to an end, shift your body weight back onto the front leg until the whole board is in contact with the snow again.

Lay-back Slide

Originally this was a classic surfing trick. It is suitable for use on banks, deep snow cornices, and on worn-out halfpipes. After the first few attempts, a somewhat steeper area can be chosen. Gliding in the fall line, you support yourself on the backside with the back hand in the snow. The board is placed diagonally in the gliding direction by pushing the tail forward with the back leg on the backside edge. The more you stretch your back leg, the more stylized this trick becomes. By flexing the back leg, the point of the board is steered back in the direction of the fall line. The upper body is brought above the board again, by forcefully pushing yourself off the snow with your back hand. The lay-back slide is completed.

Nose Roll 180°

Taken from the skateboarding kick-turn, the nose roll 180° is a demanding basic trick. It is also good preparation for airs to fakie over jumping hills. Start out in the basic position with moderate speed. By shifting your body weight forward and stretching your legs, the tail will lift out of the snow. Execute an upper-body rotation in the swing direction. The board will turn on the nose and follow the upper-body rotation. The turn is continued up to 180°. With the same amount of pressure put on both legs, the board lands on the snow. The impact is cushioned by lowering the body.

Tail Roll 180°

This skateboard kickturn is a more demanding basic maneuver. It serves as preparation for 180° airs over jumping hills that start with a fakie (gliding backwards). In a bent posture, start the fakie in the fall line. Shifting the weight onto the back leg and stretching the body forces the nose to lift out of the snow. When this happens, do an upper-body rotation in the swing direction. The board turns on the tail and follows the upper-body rotation. The turn is continued up to 180°. Even pressure is put on both legs as the board lands in the snow. The impact is cushioned by lowering the body.

Ollie

This demanding maneuver was invented by skateboarders. However, because both legs are attached to the snowboard, it does not have the same degree of difficulty it has in skateboarding. The ollie is excellently suited for jumps high in the air, even from small bumps. The ollie starts in a low basic position. At the beginning of the ride, the body weight is gradually shifted onto the back leg. By explosively stretching the legs, pressure is taken from the board. The front leg is pulled up and jerks the nose upwards. The jump is enhanced by forcefully pushing off with the back leg over the tail and yanking up the arms. A maximal flexing of both legs and a simultaneous forward bend of the upper body ensures that sufficient height is reached. The board begins to move into a flat position at the highest point. The landing takes place with even pressure on both legs, cushioned by lowering the body in stages.

Airs over the Jumping Hill

The first requirement of a perfect jump is a safe jump-off and a safe landing. Therefore, you don't have to use a ski-jumping hill for your first attempts. A small bump is sufficient for the first jump-offs and landings. As you feel more and more secure, you will reach the desired height. The jumping hill is approached in the bent basic position. The arms are spread out laterally in front of the upper body. Face the jumping hill. The jump-off is initiated by strongly pushing yourself off with both legs. Depending on the jumping hill, the legs are either completely straight (flat jump-off spot), or they are kept flexed (steep jump-off-spot). Jerking up the arms can support the jump-off. Before each landing, the legs are stretched somewhat, in order to be able to cushion the following jump-off by lowering the body. The board should be positioned parallel to the flight direction. The arms are spread out laterally in front of the upper body to maintain balance.

Backscratcher
After the ollie, the backscratcher is the next jump to learn. It is one of the few jumps that do not come from skateboarding. This trick was brought over from skiing. The style of the jump depends on how you arch and stretch your legs. You jump off by evenly pushing the legs off of the jumping-hill platform. The lower legs are flexed laterally towards the bottom. The front hand reaches for the board at the top of the front binding. The sole of the board is now vertically in the air. The maximal arch has been reached. For the landing, the board is released from the hand, and the legs are straightened. Face the landing spot. Lowering the body with the knees cushions the impact of the landing. The arms remain spread for balance.

69

Slob Air

The slob air is a basic trick in the snowboard air program. At a sufficient height, it can be twisted, or tweaked to an extreme degree. As with the ollie, you need a strong push off over the tail at the jump-off. The front leg is pulled up, and the nose is brought close to the upper body. After turning the front shoulder inwards, the front hand reaches for the nose, pulling the board at the frontside edge towards the body. The back leg is completely straight. By arching and leaning forward, stable flight is achieved. For the landing, the front leg is stretched again somewhat. Equal pressure is put on both legs in the landing. Lowering the body cushions the impact of the landing. For better balancing, the arms should be held laterally in front of the body.

Tailgrab

The tailgrab belongs in the basic program of every freestyler. It can be styled differently by using many grasp variations in the tail area. The simplest grab, shown here, is the one on the frontside edge in the tail area. The jump-off is initiated out of a slightly bent basic position. The upper body is somewhat bent backwards, and the legs are straightened. By pulling up the back leg, the nose is moved backwards and the tail upwards, towards the body. The back hand grabs the frontside edge and pulls the tail up to the hip, facing the landing spot. The board is released and returned to a flat position. The body is brought into an upright position for the landing. Lowering the body will cushion the impact.

Backside Tweak Air

The best-known snowboarding air is the backside tweak air, also called the tweaked backside air. This jump comes from the field of skating. By tweaking (twisting) the body, the jump can become extremely styled. After starting in the bent basic position, the legs are straightened at the jump-off. The body weight is shifted slightly to the tail, and the front leg is pulled up at the same time. This brings the nose in the direction of the body. The front hand grabs the nose on the backside edge. The board is held in front of the body. The hand pulls the nose in front of the body, diagonally downwards. This is the tweaked position. Facing the landing spot, the board is brought below the body by flexing the legs. The impact is cushioned by lowering the body.

Tuck Knee

For the tuck knee, a style variation of the basic frontside air, the back leg has to have a lot of freedom of movement. Therefore, the back binding should be set very loosely. The jump-off takes place evenly from both legs. The legs are pulled up, and the board is grabbed with the back hand between the bindings at the frontside edge. The pelvis is pushed forward, and the back knee is pushed against the front binding as much as possible. For the landing, let go of the board, bring it directly under the body and release the body from the squatting position. The impact is cushioned by lowering the body.

73

Iguana Back Flip

The jump, created by Damian Sanders, is a combination of a backwards somersault and a nosebone. This spectacular trick is often shown in movies, but it can be very dangerous and should only be practised after you have mastered the simple back flip. The jump needs high speed in order to get as long a rotation as possible. The backward rotation is initiated with a strong jump-off over the tail, bent knees, and a jerky shifting of the body weight backwards. The upper body leans towards the tail. During the rotation, the sequence of movements of the nosebone takes place. The back hand reaches for the frontside edge at about the level of the back binding. The front leg is boned, or twisted, automatically. Now, you lean

backwards as far as possible with the upper body. As is customary in the backward somersault, the head is pulled into the nape of the neck as far back as possible. In order to estimate the remaining time, the ground is sighted. The board is released from the back hand, the legs are pulled up, and the somersault movement is completed. By stretching the body, a continuation of the rotation is prevented, and the board is placed in a horizontal position for the landing. Lowering the body cushions the landing.

HALFPIPE
Ready for take-off

Gliding in the half-pipe is the most spectacular form of snowboarding. The thrill and the play with gravity are fascinating in this variation. Everyone who is addicted to adrenaline will enjoy the halfpipe immensely. More and more snowboarders want to experience this feeling, which resembles floating in the air. Tricks, which cause a tingling feeling in the stomach when watched, belong in the standard program. The halfpipe demands conditioning and excellent coordination. The path high in the air can only be reached with a lot of patience and practice. Therefore, the beginner should not be discouraged by initial failures. Begin with simple tricks and slowly enhance the degree of difficulty. The beginner has to be aware that falling is part of the sport, and that knowing how to fall safely is a basic requirement. If you master the fall technique (see p. 30), gliding in the vertical is not as dangerous as it looks.

The halfpipe competition has developed as part of the freestyle competition. The halfpipe is executed in a half tube form with an inclination angle of 11° to 22° in the fall line. The inner sides (walls) are concave to vertical; the bottom (flat) remains flat. Every glider shows the judges a freestyle run. Qualification for the finals consists of two runs. Sixteen men and eight women can qualify. The finals take place in three runs. The degree of difficulty, height and variation of the jumps, precision of execution, and individual style are the determining factors in scoring. Permanent classification of the tricks according to degree of difficulty and technique do not exist yet. Actually, they should not be developed, since then the individuality of this competition would get lost!

Before the first airs are jumped in the halfpipe, it is important for the snowboarder to develop a feeling for gliding in this tube. Riding safely down the walls in curves should be the first exercise. The curve radii are kept small to control the speed. Ride in a bent basic position. The curves are initiated by releasing pressure from the board by straightening the body. The board follows the course of the wall and is turned until the nose points towards the flat part of the pipe.

In the second exercise, you ride up the wall in the bent basic position until the nose points above the coping. By quickly stretching the legs, you jump off the wall. After turning the whole body towards the transition, the board follows. Facing the landing spot, the impact is cushioned by lowering the body.

In the following paragraphs, the most important halfpipe tricks are described. These can be divided into airs, inverts, and spin tricks. Frontside and backside are considered as the starting directions for the individual tricks. A frontside jump-off takes place from the frontside edge; a backside jump-off from the backside edge.

Frontside Airs

Frontside Air

The frontside air and the backside air are the basic jumps for all the following tricks. There is no way around this air, which was created by Tony Alva in skateboarding. For the beginner, the frontside air is the optimal way to get started, because the jump-off is easier on the frontside edge. When this trick is done by a very good jumper, the height and jumping range are very impressive. Start out by riding the wall in the bent basic position. Shortly before the coping is reached, push yourself off the frontside edge by strongly flexing your legs. Bring the board towards your body by pulling up your legs. Your back hand is led to the frontside edge and grabs the board between the bindings. The nose turns in the direction of the transition through the trajectory (determined by the shape of the wall) and by leaning slightly inwards. Release the board and prepare for the landing by stretching your legs and facing the landing spot. The landing is cushioned by lowering the body.

Frontside Airs

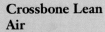

Crossbone Lean Air

From the skateboard trick developed by Neil Blender, snowboarders created several style variations, including the lean air. You can do this trick normally, nosebone, or—as shown here—crossbone. Start out in the bent basic position. In order to reach the necessary height and to be sure that the tail does not get caught at the coping, choose a steep descent. Shortly before the coping is reached, stretch your legs and jump off the frontside edge. The front leg is pulled up, and the front hand is brought to the nose on the side of the backside edge. The board is grabbed there. The upper body goes into a lateral arching position. The front arm pushes the nose away from the body. With sufficient height, this tweaked position can be held until you reach the highest point of the trajectory. For the landing, the arching posture is released, and the upper body is bent. By pulling up the legs, the board is brought back below the body. The front hand releases the board. A slight stretch of the legs initiates the landing. The landing in the transition is cushioned by bending the knees.

81

Frontside Airs

Frontside Nosebone

The frontside nose-bone is a basic frontside air as well as a variation of the normal frontside air. Start out on the wall in the bent basic position. Shortly before the coping, jump off on the frontside edge. The body weight is shifted to the back leg, which is slightly pulled up. The front leg is stretched forward. The back hand reaches between the bindings to the front-side edge and pulls the board towards the body. The back leg is pulled up as much as possible, and the front leg is stretched as much as possible. By pulling up the front leg, the board is brought back below the body. The landing in the transition is cush-ioned by lowering the body.

Frontside Airs

Chicken Salad
This trick, a variation of the frontside nosebone, is impressive because of the difficult grab, which should be practised first on the ground. With the front hand, reach from the front through the legs for the backside edge. Start out on the wall in the bent basic position. You will need a steep angle in order to reach the height necessary for the styling of this trick. Shortly before the coping, jump off strongly from the frontside edge and the tail. Immediately after the jump-off, the back hand reaches between the legs in the direction

of the backside edge. By pulling up the back leg, the board is brought close to the body. The backside edge is grabbed between the bindings. The back hand pulls back at the same time, so that the front leg is stretched, and the board is pushed forward. The upper body is bent forward as much as possible. For the landing, the nose cannot be behind the coping, or there is the risk of hanging up on it. By pulling up the front leg, the board is brought below the body. The back hand releases the board. The landing is cushioned by lowering the body.

Backside Airs

Mute Air

The mute air is an excellent way for a beginner to learn backside airs in the halfpipe. The board remains almost in the normal trajectory, and it is not styled in the opposite direction. When starting out on the wall in the bent basic position, you can choose the angle you

want. After a strong jump-off from the backside edge, the front leg is pulled up, bringing the nose closer to the body. The front hand grabs the frontside edge of the nose and pulls it to the body. The back leg is completely stretched. For the landing, release the board and bring it back under the body by pulling up both legs. Face the landing spot. Cushion the landing by lowering the body.

Backside Airs

Method Air

This classic trick, another skateboard trick, should be included in every snowboarder's program. Depending on the individual style, this trick is often confused with a tweaked backside air. Therefore, the board should have a clear, tabletop position in the air. When jumped correctly, this trick always causes a sensation because of the height and jumping range. In order to get a long trajectory, don't start out too steeply on the wall. From the bent basic position, jump off dynamically via the backside edge and the tail. After the jump-off, the body bends towards the frontside. By pulling up the legs, the board is brought to the body. The front hand grabs the frontside edge in the nose area. By stretching the legs and pulling the board towards the body with the front hand, a maximal body arch is achieved. The board is now in the tabletop position. The body is in an almost horizontal position. For the landing, the legs are pulled up, the board is brought horizontally below the body, and the upper body is bent strongly forward. The hand releases the board for the landing. Lowering the body cushions the landing.

Backside Airs

Tai Pan

The tai pan stands out because of its unusual grab. This distinguishes it from the tuck knee (shown in the chapter on hill jumping). Start out as in the mute air. A strong jump-off from the back leg ensures that sufficient height is reached—a requirement for this complicated grab. Immediately after the jump-off, the legs are pulled up, and

the board is brought closer to the body. At the same time, the front hand reaches between the bindings from behind to the frontside edge. By pulling the board against the legs, the jump is styled. Before the landing, the hand releases the board, and the body is slightly straightened until the board is below the body. Lower the body for the landing.

Backside Tailgrab

This skateboard trick is being done more frequently on the snowboard halfpipe. After a strong jump-off out of the basic position from the backside edge, the legs are pulled up. The board comes closer to the body and is grabbed at the tail with the back hand, pulling it even closer to the body. The back leg automatically flexes more strongly; the front leg is actively stretched. In order to balance the shift of weight towards the tail, the upper body is strongly bent forward. By pulling up the front leg, the board is brought below the body. The grab is released, and the board is landed on the transition with a slight stretch of the legs. Lowering the body cushions the impact.

Backside Airs

Airs to Fakie

For these tricks, you ride forward up the wall and land backwards. They should

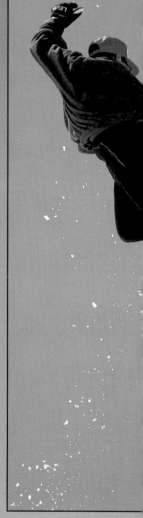

Backside Tweak to Fakie

An air landed in the fakie method is usually executed on the frontside wall. That way, the descent and the difficult fakie landing take place on the safe frontside edge. Therefore, the air has to be styled as a backside air. In the bent basic position, ride the wall on the frontside edge. The jump-off takes place with a strong stretch of the body from the frontside edge. If possible, keep your eye on the coping during the entire jump. The front leg is slightly pulled up to bring the nose closer to the body. The front hand reaches for the frontside edge of the

not be confused with fakie airs, which start out backwards and are landed forward. Almost all tricks can be landed "to fakie." Therefore, only one of these tricks is described here. Mastery of backwards gliding on the slope is required. The nose roll 180° is also a good practice exercise.

nose and pulls it in front of the body, while the back leg is stretched. This is the tweaked position. After the return point, the tweaked position is surrendered. The legs are pulled up, the board is released and brought below the body, and you face the coping. The body weight is evenly distributed on both legs. The legs are slightly stretched, and the board is landed in the transition in this position. Weight is put on the frontside edge immediately by lowering the body, cushioning the impact.

Inverts

All jumps in which the head is lower than the board during the trick are called inverts.

Hoho Plant Backside

This handplant comes from skating, but there it is only done for fun and does not count as part of the official program. In snowboarding, this is the way to start to learn the "real" handplants. The goal is a safe landing with the hands at the height of the coping, so that you don't slide down into the transition. Steep walls and an extremely steep descent on the wall make the trick easier. Start out on the backside wall with slightly bent legs. The upper body is shifted a little towards the tail. When the nose reaches the coping, jerk the body up towards the tail.

Face the envisioned landing spot for the hands. Push the board off the coping as forcefully as possible with the tail. The arms and legs are stretched completely when the handstand position is reached. For the landing, the legs have to be flexed at the hip, in order to bring the board closer to the body. An upright position is reached by forcefully pushing yourself up with your hands. Ride out of the transition in the bent basic position.

Andrecht Handplant

This handplant variation was created by the American skater, Dave Andrecht. You should master the hoho handplant before trying this trick. The pipe should not be too icy or too soft, because it is easy to slip off when landing on one hand. Start out on the backside wall extremely steeply. When the nose has reached the coping, the upper body is jerked towards the tail. The board shoots beyond the coping, and the upper body moves downward. The back arm stretches towards the coping, while the front hand reaches towards the backside edge in the direction of the nose.

The back arm is stretched and supports itself on the coping. When the board is exactly overhead and the center of gravity is reached, the legs are slightly flexed, and you grab the board with the front hand. The trick is held as long as possible in this position. By tilting the hips and releasing the backside edge, the board is quickly brought below the body. When the board is in contact with the snow again, the back hand pushes itself off the coping. In a bent position, glide out of the transition.

Inverts

Miller Flip

This trick, developed by the American Darrel Miller, is also a handplant variation from skateboarding. Along with the elguerial, described on the next page, the Miller flip is one of the most demanding jump combinations. For this trick, a wall with a lot of vertical wall space is advantageous. Start out on the frontside wall, steeply in the bent basic position. Jerk the upper body to the tail when the coping is reached. The front arm reaches for the coping. The board is flung over the coping by forcefully pushing off the tail. This brings it towards the back hand. While the front hand supports itself against the cop-

Inverts

ing, the back hand reaches between the bindings for the frontside edge. The legs are stretched, and the trick can now be held in the idle position as long as possible. With a hip turn, the board is turned above the glider with the tail towards the transition. By pulling up the legs and simultaneously bending the hips, the board is brought below the body. The back hand releases the frontside edge. By forcefully pushing off the coping with the front hand, an upright position is reached. Glide to fakie into the transition.

Elguerial

This trick is comparable to the 360° handplant, which is started with a fakie. The elguerial was originally a skater's trick, named for its inventor, Eddie Elguera. Start out on the wall, as steeply as possible, on the frontside edge in fakie. The push-off occurs after a jerky shift of the upper body towards the nose. The board is flung over the coping. The back hand (the front hand is in fakie) props itself against the coping. The legs and the board continue to turn up to the highest point; the turn is 180°. The legs are flexed somewhat, and the front hand reaches to the backside edge of the nose. The board is released and brought directly below the body by twisting the hips and pulling up the legs. The body is brought into an upright position by forcefully pushing off the coping with the back hand. In the bent position, you glide safely into the transition.

Inverts

Spin Tricks

The characteristic features of these tricks are the turns around the longitudinal and lateral axes. Three examples are explained in detail.

Frontside 360° Nosebone

The frontside 360° is the basis for all the other rotation airs, and it should be mastered first. As practice exercises, 180° airs over jumping hills are recommended. Besides the version featured here, there are numerous other grab variations for this trick. Be careful in the landing to fakie! Don't underestimate the difficulty. At the beginning, start out rather flat on the

wall to avoid a complete 360° turn. The jump-off occurs evenly with both legs from the frontside edge. The head is turned forward in the direction of the rotation (to backside) with the upper body. The back leg is pulled up, and the board is brought closer to the body. The back hand reaches for the frontside edge at the level of the back binding. The front leg is boned (turned and stretched). The board follows the continuing forward turn of the upper body. Depending on the height reached, the turn can be accelerated by pulling up the legs earlier, or the position can be held boned even longer. The back hand releases the board, the front leg is pulled up, and the board is brought back below the body. The upper body is turned towards the tail to prepare the fakie landing. In the central position, the landing is cushioned by lowering the body.

Spin Tricks

Frontside 540° Leangrab

Because of the longer spin, a higher rotation speed and more height are necessary for this trick than for the 360°. Numerous grab variations enhance the degree of difficulty of this trick. The 360°, as well as the 540°, can be jumped on the backside, but that makes them more difficult to ride because of the unusual shifting of the body weight. Start out on the wall in a flat angle. Shortly before the jump-off, the head and upper body are strongly turned forward into the rotation direction (backside). The board follows the forward turn of the upper body. The legs are flexed, and the board comes closer to the body. With the front hand, the frontside edge of the nose is grabbed and pulled towards the body. The rotation is accelerated once more. The grab is released; the board is brought below the body with a pull; and the landing spot is faced. In the last phase of the turn, it is important to stay above the board and not to lean back! Lower the body for the landing.

McTwist

This skateboard trick was developed by Mike McGill. It is one of the most difficult tricks in the snowboard half-pipe. Only a few snowboarders are capable of mastering this trick to perfection.

At high speed, start out steeply on the backside wall. When the coping is reached, the upper body is turned towards the frontside, and the front shoulder is turned in direction of the tail. By forcefully pushing off the tail, the board is flung over the coping, and the legs are brought into a squatting position. The front hand reaches for the frontside edge at the level of the front binding. The body is turned even more extremely. A rotation around the body's longitudinal axis (similar to a screw) and around the body's lateral axis (somersault) follows. Only the extreme squatting position provides the movement with enough rotation speed. (If the body opens up, a fall is unavoidable!)

The grab is released, but the tight squatting position is kept until the board is directly below the body. The landing is cushioned by lowering the body and can be corrected with the hands.

Spin Tricks

Don't overestimate your skills. Remember that a well-styled, simple air shows more skill than a botched flip.

FREERIDING

A complete nature experience — but not at the expense of nature

Freeriding is probably the most unique form of snowboarding. Riding in deep snow, the dream of every snowboarder, is a reality in freeriding. The key is "soul surfing." Here, the individualist finds his fulfillment. Wide slopes with deep snow and a boundless wintery mountain world become unforgettable moments. "Back to my roots!" The "hiking" experience, as banal as it may sound, is second spring. Long a way of life for many snowboarders in America, many European snowboarders now go this way, too. Freeriding gives everyone the opportunity to collect new impressions of nature. The surfing feeling is not the only factor. The absolute calmness and a limitless freedom are indescribable. With a small group, the snowboarder (like the skier who goes on a tour) climbs into an alpine paradise. To climb up,

snowshoes or dividable boards (which can be used as skis for the climb) are used. For tours over glacier areas, a roped party is necessary. As is the case for ski tours, alpine experience is required! If you do not have the experience, and if you are not acquainted with the area, you should only go with a guide.

So that snowboarding does no further damage to nature, every snowboarder has to follow certain rules. The following points are meant to give you some thoughts about the issue of environmental protection. If we do not take these seriously, the pleasure of gliding may soon be a thing of the past.

★ Save energy when traveling to a winter sports area.

★ Follow markings and rules.
★ Only cross through forests on marked slopes and paths.
★ Do not ride on surfaces where young trees and plants are growing.
★ Protect young trees.
★ If there is little snow, be careful not to damage the ground vegetation.
★ Do not ride over untouched slopes, if doing so might disturb wild animals.
★ Stay away from places where deer feed.
★ Take your garbage home with you.
★ Avoid loud noises. This type of snowboarding gets a bad reputation through ignorance and carelessness. Freeriding should not be confused with thought-

lessly leaving marked slopes! On the contrary, the snowboarder has to plan every little detail, take responsibility for it, and think carefully about each action. These decisions determine the degree of safety of the experience. The following points have to be followed by freeriders:
★ If you are inexperienced, only climb with a guide.
★ Climb in a group of at least three.
★ Get the current local avalanche reports.
★ Leave information about the route that you are planning to take.
★ Carry a search device for buried persons with you on each tour.
★ Enhance your own knowledge; for example, attend an avalanche class.
★ Be considerate of the forest.
Only when these points are observed can freeriding become an experience and not a danger!

THE RULES OF BEHAVIOR

The 10 International Ski Federation (FIS) Rules for the Conduct of Skiers apply to the snowboarder as they do for everyone else on the slopes. Their purpose is to avoid accidents on the piste, or downhill trail, and responsible and careful skiers (and snowboarders) are obliged to be familiar with and respect them. The FIS Rules (1990) are as follows:

1 **Respect for others**
   A skier must behave in such a way that he does not endanger or prejudice others.

2 **Control of speed and skiing**
   A skier must ski in control. He must adapt his speed and manner of skiing to his personal ability and to the prevailing conditions of terrain, snow and weather as well as to the density of traffic.

3 **Choice of route**
   A skier coming from behind must choose his route in such a way that he does not endanger skiers ahead.

4 **Overtaking**
   A skier may overtake another skier above or below and to the right or to the left provided that he leaves enough space for the overtaken skier to make any voluntary or involuntary movement.

5 **Entering and starting**
   A skier entering a marked run or starting again after stopping must look up and down the run to make sure that he can do so without endangering himself or others.

6 **Stopping on the piste**
   Unless absolutely necessary, a skier must avoid stopping on the piste in narrow places or where visibility is restricted. After a fall in such a place, a skier must move clear of the piste as soon as possible.

7 **Climbing and descending on foot**
   Both a skier climbing or descending on foot must keep to the side of the piste.

8 **Respect for signals and markings**
   A skier must respect the signals and markings.

9 **Assistance**
   At accidents, every skier is dutybound to assist.

10 **Identification**
   Every skier and witness, whether responsible party or not, must exchange names and addresses following an accident.

 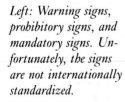

Left: Warning signs, prohibitory signs, and mandatory signs. Unfortunately, the signs are not internationally standardized.

Right above: "Closed" signs have to be followed under all circumstances.

Right below: References to slope and emergency services.

GOING ON FROM HERE

Right from the start in Europe, the development of snowboarding was influenced by the media and by industry. Instead of giving the sport enough time to develop, new companies jumped at the trendy sport and marketed it ruthlessly. The best example of that is the development of competitive snowboarding. Quickly taken up by manufacturers and the media and recognized as an advertising bonanza, the sports events were held in a totally exaggerated way. One season later, the same companies dropped the sport. The result was chaos.

The image of the professional suffers partially from false representations in the media. For example, professional competitions are announced, but amateurs are also allowed to compete. Thus, the competitive level of the professional sport is lowered and future advertisements for snowboarding competitions lose credibility. Until recently, snowboarding has suffered from these problems. However, the founding of the PSA (Professional Snowboard Association) is a step in the right direction. During the last two years, snowboarding experienced an enormous increase in participants. Many young people, especially from the cities, discovered this sport for themselves. Skateboarding, a sport which was born in large cities and which influenced snowboarding history, has had a considerable part in this pleasant upswing. But the media and the manufacturers continue to portray skateboarding in a way that does not do it justice. The lifestyle of a skater should not be portrayed as destructive and rebellious. A disastrous mistake is made when one goes into nature with this kind of hardcore image. It is not in the interest of skateboarding or snowboarding that this image is assumed by more and more young people and that it is even shown off on the slopes. A kind of pseudo-skateboard wave (by no means accepted in the relevant circles of the skateboard and snowboard scenes) has overflowed the winter sports areas. Only a small number of those who swim on this wave have ever had anything to do with serious skateboarding. But it is exactly this circle of people that brings both of these sports discredit! It is obvious that more mature people who are interested in snowboarding cannot identify themselves with these chaotic types. Surely, the winter sports areas cannot be pictured without snowboarding anymore. But if we want to pursue the goal of making this sport acceptable to the masses, snowboarding has to be made accessible for every age group. Otherwise, the sport will inevitably be placed on the shelf. The fact that snowboarding has established itself in alpine sports does not solve the problems which still exist between skiers and snowboarders. Many snowboarders forget that skiers have been in the mountains long before snowboarders, and not vice versa. Consideration and correct behavior on the slopes should be natural behavior for snowboarders.

GLOSSARY

Air: Jump in the halfpipe, over edges and bumps.

Arch: Extreme arching of the body when doing an air.

Asymmetricals: Snowboards which are constructed asymmetrically.

Back flip: Rearward somersault.
Backside: General term for rides and jumps during which pressure is put on the heel edge.
Backside wall: Wall in the halfpipe on which you start a ride on the backside edge.
Bail: Controlled fall.
Banks: Extremely flat halfpipe walls.
Bevel kit: Wedge-shaped baseplate for the binding.

Bone: Jump style in which one leg is pulled up and the other one is stretched.
Buckle: Closure for a soft binding.
Bumps: Small mounds.

Canting wedge: Metal or plastic wedge that is attached underneath the binding to help the snowboarder stand better anatomically.

Carve: Extreme curve or ride on the edge.
Coping: Upper edge of the halfpipe.
Cruise: Relaxed gliding.

Cut: Qualification for the finals in a contest.
Cut turn: Cut swing; curve is ridden on the edge.

Drop in: Expression meaning that you are next in the halfpipe.

Duct tape: An adhesive tape.

Edge: Either edge of the snowboard.
Edge length: Area of the edge that actually has contact with the snow.

Extension: Halfpipe segment that is higher than the rest of the pipe.

Fakie: Riding backwards.
Fall line: The connecting line between the highest and lowest point of a slope, thought to be the shortest line down the slope.

FIS: Federation Internationale de Ski, or International Ski Federation.
Flat: Flat surface between the walls of the halfpipe.
Flex: Bending behavior of the board, binding, boots, or body part.

Flip: Somersault.
Float: Air which is drawn out long and wide.
Frontside: General term for rides and jumps during which pressure is put on the toe edge.

Goofy: Binding position in which the right foot is in the front binding.

Grab: Grabbing the board during the jump.

Halfpipe: Tube constructed with two curved segments, permitting the snowboarder to ride back and forth.
Handplant: Trick in the halfpipe in which one hand reaches for the coping.
Hang up: Getting hung up with the board on the coping.

Hard boot: Boot for plate binding.
Hard core: The type of snowboarder who is on his board in any kind of weather.
Heel edge: Backside edge.
Heel pad: Calf padding in a shell binding.

High back: Shell binding.
High-top bindings: Shell bindings that are suitable for alpine boarding because of an additional top buckle.
Hiking: Climbing the slope on foot; making a tour with the snowboard.

I

Inserts: Threaded bolts in the board into which the screws of the binding are inserted.

Invert: An overall term for all tricks in which the head is lower than the board.

ISA: International Snowboard Association.

J

Jam: Riding fast and safely.

Judges: Judges in a contest.

K

Kick: Bend upwards.

Kicker: Good spot in the halfpipe or on the jumping hill.

Kicktail: Bent-up tail.

L

Leash: Catch strap.

Lip: Upper edge of a snow cornice, a half-pipe, or a wave.

M

Moguls: Bumps.

Mounting angle: Angle at which the binding is set in relation to the board's longitudinal axis.

N

Nose: Point of the board.

Nose kick: Degree of the shovel that is bent up.

O

Off the lip: Term from surfing, meaning turning on a snow-cornice edge.

Platform: Upper edge of the halfpipe, which is wider.
Plate binding: Snowboard binding for the hard boot.

Powder: Deep snow.
Powder session: Riding with a group in deep snow.
Pro jump: Artificial jump in the parallel slalom.

Push: By lowering the body, giving the board enough acceleration to be able to ride up the halfpipe walls.

Quarter pipe: Half a halfpipe.

Rad: Radical.
Ramp: Natural or artificial jumping hill.
Regular: Binding position in which the left foot is in the front binding.

Revert: After completing a turn, the board is turned an additional 180°, and the snowboarder rides backwards.
Rip: Riding fast and hard.

Rocker: An upward bend of the snowboard tail.
Round tail: A round tail form.
Rounded square tail: Straight tail with rounded corners.

Sandwich construction method: The three methods used for manufacturing snowboards.
Scoop: Shovel bend up.
Session: Ride in a group of snowboarders.
Shell binding: Binding for soft boots.
Shred: Riding hard.

Sidewalk: Platform.
Slam: Uncontrolled fall.
Slush: Slush snow.
Soft binding: Shell binding.
Soft boot: Boot for shell binding.
Snurfer: Predecessor of the snowboard.
Spin: Turn.
Stall: Staying as long as possible in a lip trick.

Stick: Board; landing a difficult trick.
Stiff leg: Riding with stretched legs.
Style: Individual style.
Swallowtail: V-shaped cut, specifically used in powder boards.

Tail: Rear.
Tailkick: Degree of bending of the snowboard tail.
Tension span: Degree to which a board is bent in the middle on a level surface.

Track: Path in the slalom-course.
Transition: Round part of the halfpipe; connects the flat with the coping.
Tuck: Going into the squatting position.
Turn: Curve; swing.

Tweak: Twisting; device for styling jumps.
Twist: Turn around the body's longitudinal axis.
Twisting: Twist of the lower body in the opposite direction of the upper body.

Vert: Vertical part of the wall.

Waisting: Difference between the narrowest and the widest part of a board.
Wall: Halfpipe wall.

Wind drift: Snow drift.

INDEX